MEDIA POWER

War and Conflict

Judith Anderson

FRANKLIN WATTS
LONDON•SYDNEY

First published in 2010 by
Franklin Watts
338 Euston Road
London NW1 3BH

Franklin Watts Australia
Level 17/207 Kent Street
Sydney NSW 2000

Series editor: Julia Bird
Design: Nimbus Design

A CIP catalogue record for this book is available from the British Library.

ISBN 978 0 7496 8868 4

Dewey classification: 302.2'3

Picture credits:
Zohra Bensemra/Corbis: 9; Bettmann/Corbis: 11, 28; Paul Buck/epa/Corbis: 19. CNN/Getty Images: 16; Peter Endig/DPA/PAI: 33; epa/Corbis: 32; Everett Collection/Rex Features: 21; Gleb Garanich/Reuters/Corbis: 34; Eddie Gerald/Alamy: 30; Ali Haider/epa/Corbis: 14. Ralf-Finn Hestoft/Corbis: 26; Chris Hondrus/Getty Images: front cover; Hulton-Deutsch/Corbis: 8; ICP-UK/Alamy: 40; Hamid Jalaludin/ PAI: 37; KPA/ZUMA/Rex Features: 15; Michael Macor/SF Chronicle/Corbis: 17; Gideon Mendel/Corbis: 31; Pictorial Press/Alamy: 38; Picturepoint/Topham: 10; Rex Features: 18, 24, 25; Reuters/ Corbis: 20; Patrick Robert/Corbis: 35r; Gavin Rodgers/Rex Features: 41; Ron Sachs/Corbis: 27; Murad Sezer/AP/PAI: 39; Sipa Press/Rex Features: 13, 22, 29. Mike Stewart/Sygma/Corbis: 35l; Mark St George /Rex Features: 36; John Stillwell/epa/Corbis: 23. Goran Tomasevic/Corbis: 12.

Printed in Malaysia

Franklin Watts is a division of Hachette Children's Books, an Hachette UK company.
www.hachette.co.uk

Contents

Reporting war and conflict

The media has become a familiar feature of modern warfare. Generals call press conferences. Camera crews travel with troops. Armies have media officers, while terrorists communicate online. With the arrival of digital media and 24-hour news, it can be hard to believe that conflict is actually happening unless we have the evidence on a screen in front of us.

War media

Of course, we haven't always been able to rely on 24-hour TV news or instant access to events via the Internet. Reports of battles abroad used to take weeks to reach audiences at home. The arrival of cinema newsreels and radio in the twentieth century made the details of war more accessible to many, but the information was still subject to delay and interference from governments anxious to shield voters from the horrors of the battlefield.

Winning the public over

Public opinion has always been important in any conflict. Soldiers and politicians rely on the public's belief in their cause in order to provide troops, make weapons, maintain supplies and boost morale. If public opinion wavers and support for the war begins to diminish, soldiers may be forced to withdraw or surrender. This battle for public opinion is central to understanding the power of the media in any conflict.

Photographs such as this of the Crimean War (1853–1856) were among the first actual images of war to be published.

The media as a weapon

Wars are all about taking sides. The side that uses the media most effectively is sometimes able to influence an entire conflict. Managing the media is therefore a strategic aim for many generals and politicians. But there are other influences on the media. Journalists, editors, advertisers, owners and even the audience themselves have their own opinions about the kind of coverage they want. This may have a significant impact on how a conflict is reported.

Case study: The war in Darfur

This picture shows UN peacekeeping forces in Darfur, Sudan. However, the western media rarely provides much coverage of the conflict.

Hundreds of thousands of people have died in the civil war in the Darfur region of Sudan in Africa. Yet there is relatively little coverage of it in some western media. This might be because our military involvement is limited to a few UN peacekeeping forces. It might also be due to the fact that there are fewer western reporters in Darfur, because it is very dangerous. Or it might be because the media perceive a lack of public interest in African conflicts generally.

• Up for discussion •

Most audiences around the world now have access to live, 24-hour coverage of conflicts such as the war in Afghanistan and the fighting in Israel and Gaza. What are the advantages of this for audiences and for the combatants?

Eyewitness

An eyewitness is someone who is present at an event and reports what they have seen. The media and most audiences place a high value on eyewitness accounts of violence or conflict and their words are generally accepted as true. Eyewitnesses are one of the main sources for war reporting. They 'were there'.

Vital evidence

Sometimes eyewitnesses are journalists. Sometimes they are ordinary people who write letters, keep diaries or give interviews. The experiences of innocent victims of conflict are often particularly important as evidence for 'war crimes' – crimes that go beyond military combat to include genocide or torture. The existence of the gas chambers in Nazi concentration camps in the Second World War (1939–1945), for example, may not have come to light without the evidence of the survivors and their liberators who wrote about their experiences, talked to journalists and took photographs of what remained.

Anne Frank's account of her time in hiding from the Nazis became an international best-seller after the Second World War.

The whole truth?

Eyewitness accounts don't always reveal the whole story. Did a single eyewitness see everything that happened? Do they know the circumstances that led up to that event? Probably not. Yet eyewitness accounts are often dramatic and compelling. If a TV station or a newspaper thinks it has a particularly vivid eyewitness version of events then it may over-emphasise its significance in order to attract a bigger audience.

Case study: The bombing of Nagasaki

When US planes dropped a nuclear bomb on Nagasaki in Japan in August 1945, it was witnessed by passenger William Laurence, a journalist for the New York Times. *He observed: 'We removed our glasses after the first flash but the light still lingered on, a bluish-green light that illuminated the entire sky all around. A tremendous blast wave struck [our plane] and made it tremble from nose to tail. This was followed by four more blasts in rapid succession, each resounding like the boom of cannon fire hitting our plane from all directions.' His account is vivid and real, but it does not convey what was happening on the ground when the bomb struck, or the terrible human suffering that followed.*

Around a third of Nagasaki's buildings were destroyed by the nuclear bomb and almost 74,000 people lost their lives.

• Up for discussion •

William Laurence's account of the bombing of Nagasaki does not tell the whole story of what happened that day. Does this mean his report is inaccurate? How do you think the media should treat eyewitness accounts of conflict?

In the frame

Some of the most revealing eyewitness material about conflicts around the world is found in photographic images and video sequences. Pictures provide clear visual evidence of location and participants. They show the horror and the violence and the grief on people's faces. Because of this, they have a powerful impact on audiences and are often more memorable than words.

No picture, no news

Television relies on images. Without pictures, there is nothing to look at. So camera crews and photographers are often at the front line in a conflict. They are the eyewitnesses, sending images back to newsrooms for journalists to incorporate into their news bulletins. But this can have an impact on what stories the programme decides to feature. If there are plenty of dramatic images then the story might be given more prominence. If there are no pictures available, the story might not be shown at all.

The camera never lies...

Certain types of image can have a huge impact on public opinion. In the recent war in Iraq, pictures of the toppling of a statue of the deposed president, Saddam Hussein, helped to boost the morale of US and British troops. They appeared to signal the end of an unpopular regime. However, a single image rarely tells the whole story. For what followed was chaos and civil war in a country still painfully divided.

A statue of Iraq's former president, Saddam Hussein, is pulled to the ground in Baghdad, April 2003.

Case study: The Vietnam War

The war in Vietnam in the 1960s has often been described as the first war to be shown in images. US troops were sent in to fight alongside the South Vietnamese against their enemy North Vietnam. However, because of the presence of so many photojournalists and TV crews, audiences around the world were able to see the North Vietnamese as real people, leading ordinary lives. Graphic images of suffering had a huge impact on public opinion, which eventually helped lead to a US withdrawal from the region.

Images of armed US soldiers questioning civilian Vietnamese families helped to turn public opinion against US involvement in the region.

During the conflict in Northern Ireland in the 1970s and 1980s, photographers were repeatedly accused of encouraging youths to throw stones at British soldiers in an attempt to create the images of confrontation that were popular with British and Irish newspapers.

• *Up for discussion* •

Do you think the presence of a photographer at the scene of a conflict can affect what happens next? Why?

Some images of war can be quite shocking. Do you think that they really help to show people what war is like? Why? Or do they just sell newspapers?

An impartial view?

Some media organisations deliberately support a particular point of view, aiming to reflect the politics or the beliefs of specific audiences. Other news networks, newspapers and websites claim to have a policy of impartial reporting. This usually means balanced reporting – reporting that is not biased in favour of one side or another. But in any conflict, impartiality is a difficult thing to achieve.

No access

Balanced reporting means making sure that different points of view are given equal emphasis. It means providing news from both sides in any conflict. However, often journalists are not able (or not allowed) to access all areas in a war zone, so they have to base their reporting on limited evidence. Or they rely on the military or politicians to tell them what has happened. In the absence of other evidence, journalists may also speculate on what *might* have happened in the conflict.

US Colonel Marc Ferraro holds a press conference to report developments in the conflict in Iraq.

Case study: Conflict in the Middle East

Foreign journalists were forced to report on the Gaza bombardment from a hilltop on the Israeli border.

The bitter conflict between Israel and the Palestinian people continues to present huge challenges for news media and audiences around the world. On the one hand, Israel is a tiny country and it must defend itself against bombs and suicide attacks from Palestinians and others. On the other hand, Israel has huge military resources and sometimes uses them against ordinary Palestinians living in overcrowded areas like Gaza, on its border. The shared history of these two sides is painful and complex. Both accuse the international media of bias, or a failure to convey people's point of view.

At the end of 2008, Israel began to bomb Gaza in response to Palestinian militants who had been attacking Israel. But Gaza is densely populated, and the militants live amongst ordinary Palestinians. Anticipating intense media interest in the number of civilian casualties, Israel stopped most journalists from entering Gaza. So journalists were forced to report from the Israeli side of the border where Palestinians were retaliating with rocket fire. The full reality of the Gaza bombardment was not seen. However, some journalists did manage to report from inside Gaza, including staff of Al Jazeera TV and the BBC's Palestinian producer Rushdi Abu Alouf.

• Up for discussion •

Some people argue that it is impossible for any journalist or news organisation to be entirely impartial. What do you think?

When a TV appeal was launched to raise aid for the victims of Gaza, the BBC refused to show it on the grounds that such an appeal would damage its impartiality. Others disagreed. What do you think?

Embedded reporting

One way to report on a war is to follow soldiers into battle. Journalists sometimes join a military combat unit as a way to get close to the action. This is known as embedded reporting. The journalist lives with a group of soldiers and observes them on the front line in order to relay the experience to audiences around the world.

The soldier's experience

The advantages of embedded reporting are that the public gets to see how soldiers live and how they carry out their duties. It helps to show the human face of combat troops and explains the pressures they are under. How does it feel to be caught in a sandstorm in a tank? What's it like to come under fire? Such reporting can do a great deal to boost public support for the work of the armed forces.

A limited view

However, some people feel that embedded reporters are not properly independent or impartial. They see only one side of the conflict, and their experiences are carefully managed and controlled by military commanders. Martin Bell, a former BBC journalist, has argued that 'reporters are driven back into green zones [heavily guarded 'safe' areas] and fortified compounds where they no longer have a function as eyewitnesses... Embedded reporting is so limited in scope that it serves as little more than a recruiting movie.'

Embedded reporters can in theory report directly from a war's front line of combat.

Case study: Embedded in Iraq

During the Iraq war, the US military introduced a mass 'embed' programme for journalists in the war zone. From their point of view, it was good for public relations because it made soldiers look human and allowed them to display their military power and professionalism. It also meant that journalists faced less risk to their own safety. Yet many embedded journalists were criticised for spending so much time with troops that they became more like fellow soldiers than impartial journalists, while non-embedded journalists were not allowed the same level of access to areas of conflict.

Journalists wait to join their assigned military units before the invasion of Iraq in March 2003.

• Up for discussion •

Why is it important for journalists to be able to move freely in a war zone?

What do you think Martin Bell meant when he said that embedded reporting served 'as little more than a recruiting movie'?

Spinning the story

The military don't just rely on embedded journalists to tell their side of the story. They also hold press conferences and put out press releases via their own media officers. This helps them to manage the flow of information. However, the military are participants in a war, so it is unlikely that their viewpoint is entirely objective.

Good publicity: a US soldier hands out colouring books and sweets to local children.

Spin

Sometimes the military may put a 'spin' on a news story. This may mean emphasising the advantages of a strategy while playing down the disadvantages, or turning bad news into a more positive story.

Case study: The Allies in Iraq – friends or enemies?

The Allied forces that invaded Iraq in 2003 were keen to be regarded as liberators and friends of ordinary Iraqis. In order to spread this view, they invited the media to watch them hand out sweets and toys to local children and food parcels to displaced civilians. Similarly, the Allies occasionally tried to spin stories about stray bombs landing on the homes of civilians, arguing that the damage and loss of life might have been caused by Iraqi fire. However, some news media consistently challenged this version of events.

A willing media

The media, hungry for news and keen to access images, has been accused of accepting military 'spin' too readily. In wartime, when information can be difficult to access, it can be easier to accept the story as it is handed out at a press conference. However, it isn't just the military who 'spin' news. When the media published shocking pictures of US soldiers torturing Iraqi detainees at Abu Ghraib prison, talk show host Rush Limbaugh tried to spin the story by arguing that the soldiers were just 'having a good time'.

Bad publicity: photos of US soldier Lynndie England abusing and torturing Iraqi detainees at Abu Ghraib prison in 2003 created a media storm.

• *Up for discussion* •

'The first casualty in war is truth', according to some commentators. Do you think this is fair, or true? Is it unpatriotic of journalists to draw the public's attention to the failings of their own soldiers? What's your view?

Gotcha?

Some media organisations regularly put their own 'spin' on a news story. When British troops sank the Argentine ship *General Belgrano* during the Falklands War in 1982, *The Sun* newspaper published pictures alongside a headline that said 'GOTCHA'. It was toned down in later editions to 'Did 1,500 Argies Drown?' as the scale of the loss of life became apparent.

Propaganda

Propaganda means using the media to promote a particular point of view. It is more than a response to events; it is a deliberate attempt to manipulate public opinion, justify a country's actions and promote hatred of the enemy. Propaganda may be used by a government, or the military, or by those who oppose them.

The battle for hearts and minds

Propaganda relies on the media to spread its message. During the Second World War, a character known as Lord Haw Haw made regular radio broadcasts from Nazi Germany to British and American listeners. The purpose of these broadcasts was to demoralise Allied troops and the general public by exaggerating their losses in order to bring about their surrender. Similarly, during the Iraq war, the US sent emails to top Iraqi officials asking them to change sides. The Iraqi president Saddam Hussein shut down access to the Internet as a result.

Case study: Saving Private Lynch

In April 2003 in Iraq, the vehicle in which US Private Jessica Lynch was travelling was ambushed by Iraqi forces and she was captured alive. Iraqi soldiers took her to a local hospital and held her there for eight days before she was found by US special forces. Their 'daring' rescue was captured in a short film that was broadcast around the world. The US military said that Lynch had been shot and abused during her ordeal and the media proclaimed her an American hero.

However, when Lynch was able to speak for herself, she revealed a different story. She had not been shot or abused, the Iraqi soldiers left the hospital before she was rescued and she was treated well by hospital staff.

Creating a myth

Propagandists have often used images or films to inspire people or make them afraid. *Battleship Potemkin* was one of the first ever propaganda films, made in Russia in 1925 to encourage world revolution. Nowadays, suicide bombers video themselves talking about their desire to be martyrs in order to persuade others to join them (see p.27). The Internet in particular has the power both to create propaganda and to spread its message rapidly around the world. Its content is largely unregulated, allowing interest groups to publish whatever truths (or lies) best suit their purpose.

• Up for discussion •

Why did the US military film Jessica Lynch's rescue (see case study, left) and release it to the media?

Do you think there are any circumstances in which propaganda is acceptable during wartime?

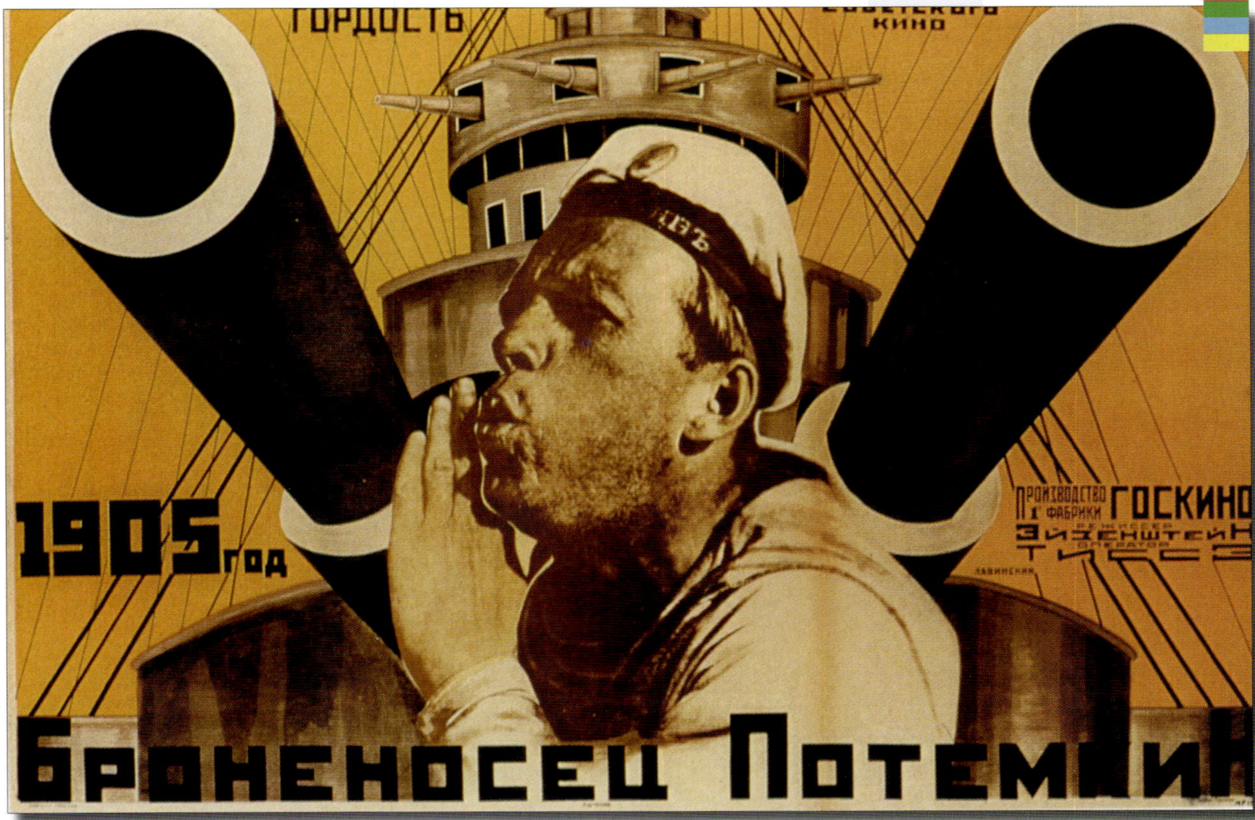

A poster for the film *Battleship Potemkin* which glorified rebellion and revolution.

Censorship

A news blackout, or censorship, occurs when journalists and editors are prevented from publishing or broadcasting a particular story. Blackouts are usually imposed by the government or the military during wartime to protect sensitive information and save lives. Sometimes the media agrees to this voluntarily. However, sometimes it is forced on them.

Laws on censorship

Most countries have laws to protect against the publication of sensitive military information such as troop deployment or battle strategy. Few people would argue about the need to keep people safe, but in recent years many questions have been raised about the content of new anti-terror laws in the US, the UK and elsewhere. These appear to limit the media's freedom to report on the speeches and activities of terrorist organisations in the wake of the terrorist attacks of 9/11 (see p.25). Nevertheless, the Internet remains relatively immune to such laws. All sorts of sensitive or secret information makes its way onto websites through 'leaks' or anonymous postings. Because of this, many have come to regard the Internet as the champion of free speech.

Silencing the opposition

In some countries censorship is particularly heavy-handed, usually in

Elections in Iran in 2009 were followed by violent protests after accusations of corruption. Iran's strict censorship laws meant that people took to the Internet forum Twitter to share their images of the protests.

order to silence the opposition and stop 'difficult' news from spreading. For example, China has frequently tried to impose a news blackout in Tibet because it fears what will happen if people learn about the protests against Chinese rule there. Nowadays it is getting harder to enforce a news blackout as more and more people are able to access the media via satellite or mobile phone or email. Nevertheless, the poorest or most remote communities in the world can still be 'cut off' from events.

Case study: Prince Harry in Afghanistan

Prince Harry, third in line to the British throne, is a serving soldier who was sent to Afghanistan in 2008. Before his departure from the UK, however, a voluntary news blackout was negotiated with the British media, who agreed not to report his deployment in exchange for interviews with him that they could use once his tour was over. The blackout was made to protect the prince and those around him who might have become targets if his presence was made public. However, after ten weeks the story was leaked on a US website. The media blackout was lifted and Prince Harry was forced to return to the UK.

Prince Harry's deployment in Afghanistan was made possible by the agreement of a media blackout.

• Up for discussion •

Is an unregulated Internet the champion of free speech or a threat to national security? What's your view?

Do you think the British media were right to agree to a news blackout for Prince Harry in Afghanistan? What about the foreign journalists who finally revealed the story?

The terrorist's tool

Terrorism is any act of violence designed to spread fear among the general population. It is commonly used to draw attention to the terrorists' aims, or to force a government to give in to their political or ideological demands. To do this effectively, terrorism often relies on the media.

Media benefits

When a terrorist's bomb is detonated, killing innocent members of the public and causing chaos and disruption to transport and communications systems, the media has a big story on its hands. People want information about what has taken place. They want pictures, explanations and analysis. And the media depends on a constant supply of dramatic news if it is to keep its audience interested. However, some people argue that by broadcasting such details the media is simply publicising the terrorists' demands and profiting from their evil actions.

The IRA and the media

The IRA (Irish Republican Army) deliberately targeted civilians in its bombing campaigns in Ireland and the UK during the 1960s–1980s. It wanted to end British rule in Northern Ireland and believed that news of the suffering it inflicted would generate so much fear among the general public that the pressure would force the British government to withdraw. Certainly, images like that of the Omagh bombing in 1998 frightened and worried people. But in the end it was negotiation, not terror, that brought about change.

The aftermath of an IRA bomb in Omagh, Northern Ireland, in 1998.

Case study: 9/11

The militant Islamic group al Qaeda was responsible for the terrorist attacks on New York and the Pentagon of 11 September 2001. The terrorists' aim was to spread fear through maximum media coverage and in this they were very successful. When two hijacked planes crashed into the Twin Towers in New York, several thousand people lost their lives but millions more watched in horror as TV images of the explosions and the collapsing towers were broadcast live around the world. In the days that followed, the footage was replayed endlessly, but some people felt uncomfortable about its effects on the general public. A few TV channels decided to show still images to limit the publicity they were giving the terrorists. Similar doubts were expressed over video footage of al Qaeda leader Osama Bin Laden.

The 9/11 terrorists knew that the Twin Towers in New York were highly visible buildings with plenty of TV crews already in the vicinity, ensuring maximum coverage of the attacks.

• Up for discussion •

Would the attack on the Twin Towers have had the same impact if it had not been filmed by camera crews and members of the public? Why?

Choose your words

The power of the media to influence public opinion is partly due to the stories it chooses to cover and from which angle or point of view. But one of its most powerful and subtle tools is language itself. Which words will a journalist use to describe people who launch an attack, for example? Are they soldiers, martyrs, militants, freedom fighters or terrorists? Each term carries its own meaning and will have a different impact on the audience.

Reducing the impact

When things go wrong in a conflict, public support for the military or the government may start to decline. So in order to turn the attention away from the human suffering, words are chosen to reduce its impact. During the invasion of Iraq, the US military referred to civilian casualties as 'collateral damage'. Those media organisations that most strongly supported the invasion used this phrase in their reports. Other journalists preferred to refer to the dead and hurt in more direct terms.

An emotional response

Sometimes sections of the media want to sensationalise an event because it makes a better story and attracts bigger audiences. Politicians do

Timothy McVeigh carried out a bombing that killed 168 people in Oklahoma in 1995, including 19 children. He described the children's deaths as 'collateral damage'.

this too, in order to gain public support for military action. So words like 'bloodbath' or 'massacre' or 'martyr' or 'hero' may be used as they create an emotional response in people, even if the words are an exaggeration or distortion of the truth.

Sound bites

The media may also use a phrase because it provides them with a hook or a headline in as few words as possible. The term 'axis of evil' was first used by former US President George W. Bush to describe the nuclear threat from Iraq, Iran and North Korea. It provided the media with a memorable 'sound bite' and was repeated in news bulletins over and over again.

• *Up for discussion* •

Suicide bombers like Mohammed Siddique Khan, who blew up a London train in 2005, often call themselves 'martyrs'. What sort of response does this provoke in you? Do you think that this is the effect they intend?

Case study: The global war on terror

The phrase 'global war on terror' was first used to describe the response of the US and its allies to the terrorist attacks of 11 September, 2001 (see p.25). It was quickly taken up by most media outlets as a strong phrase with clear associations. However, when it was used to justify the invasion of Iraq, which was not connected with specific terrorist groups, people began to question it. The UK Director of Public Prosecutions argued that terrorists are criminals, not soldiers, and that therefore it is inappropriate to speak of a 'war' against them. When US President Obama took office in 2009, he chose to refer to 'overseas contingency operations' instead of 'the war on terror' and the term was quietly dropped.

US President George W. Bush coined the phrase a 'global war on terror' in a speech following the al Qaeda attacks on New York and the Pentagon on 11 September, 2001.

Stirring up hatred

Most of the time we think of the media as being relatively independent. This independence is important in democratic countries, where people are free to express different opinions. However, in some countries the media is controlled by those who wish to stir up public hatred for minority groups.

Nazi Germany

Sometimes governments go beyond censorship and use their power to put across their propaganda in a single-minded way that leaves no room for opposition or debate. When German leader Adolf Hitler commissioned the director Leni Riefenstahl to make a film called *Triumph of the Will* in 1934, his intention was to promote and glorify Nazi military might at the expense of non-Nazis within Germany and abroad. Hitler was a skilled propagandist and his speeches calling for racial purity and anti-semitism were widely broadcast on radio and in films, laying the groundwork for his 'Final Solution', or the extermination of the Jewish people.

Leni Riefenstahl directs a scene from *Triumph of the Will* in Nuremberg, Germany, in 1934.

Inciting violence

Other leaders have also used the media in this way. During the wars in the Balkans in central Europe in the 1990s, the Serbian leader Slobodan Milosevic used state-controlled TV to incite Serb hatred of ethnic minorities. More recently, however, fears have been expressed that an independent, unregulated media can also be used to stir up hatred. In the UK, for example, laws have been introduced to limit the freedom of militant groups to express their hatred of democratic values or incite violence. Those banned from entering the country under these laws have included militant Islamists, neo-Nazis and animal rights extremists. However, shutting down extremist websites is proving more difficult.

Case study: Genocide in Rwanda, Africa

Between April and June 1994, more than 800,000 Rwandans were killed in a wave of unprecedented violence that broke out between the rival Hutu and Tutsi ethnic groups. Most of the dead were from the Tutsi minority. The violence was sparked by the shooting-down of the Rwandan president's plane, but tension between the two groups was nothing new. Many witnesses reported that Hutu radio propaganda had encouraged the killings by blaming Tutsis for the country's problems, suggesting that Tutsis were themselves planning an attack and promising that Hutus would be able to take the land of any Tutsis they killed.

• *Up for discussion* •

Which is more important – preserving freedom of speech, or preventing people from inciting hatred and violence through the media? Why?

Would the Rwandan violence have been less extreme if ordinary people had greater access to TV and the Internet? What do you think?

Hutu civilians prepare for violence with wooden guns.

A moral duty

Journalists who observe war in person are often witness to terrible events. Many people think that they have a professional obligation to describe what takes place as accurately as possible. But what if a journalist witnesses a murder, torture or a war crime? What if they see something that goes against the usual 'rules' of engagement? Should they intervene?

A neutral position

Journalists attempting to remain neutral for the sake of objectivity often find themselves in a difficult position. Audiences react strongly to images of suffering or injustice and sometimes people ask why the TV crews don't stop filming and start helping. But if journalists get involved or demand change their objectivity is lost, and the military may start to question their presence, denying them access or even seeing them as targets for violence. Many journalists argue that the evidence itself provides a crucial voice for those who are suffering.

Testifying in court

During the 1990s, journalists from many countries observed the wars in the Balkans at first hand. When the conflict ended, a war crimes tribunal was set up in The Hague to establish what had taken place and to decide whether anyone was guilty of the crimes of genocide or ethnic cleansing. A number of foreign journalists were called to give evidence, but some refused, arguing that it would expose those informants to whom they had promised anonymity.

War journalists often have to work fast in rapidly changing, dangerous situations. They don't have time to get involved.

Case study: The media and Rwanda

One of the many disturbing aspects of the killings in Rwanda in 1994 (see p.29) was the absence of media reports about what was happening. Some people have accused journalists of misinterpreting the bloodshed as 'tribal violence' and failing to recognise that it was organised genocide. On the other hand, when pictures of the violence started to filter out of the country, some editors and news managers refused to show them on the grounds that they were too distressing for their audiences. So for three weeks that April, the massacres failed to make foreign news bulletins. It wasn't until June that the full horror was reported in the media and by then, an estimated 500,000 Tutsis were already dead.

Dancille Nyirabazungu, whose five children were killed during the massacres, stands in front of victims' skulls in a church in Kigali, Rwanda.

• Up for discussion •

Some people think the media's main responsibility is towards the interests of its audience. Others think the media has a duty to reveal the truth at any cost. What do you think?

In the line of fire

People working in the media can themselves become targets in a conflict. Soldiers or police may attack journalists and film crews in order to stop an investigation or send out a warning to the media to stay away. Militants and extremists may target them as representatives of 'the enemy'. Sometimes even ordinary civilians attack them because they are suspicious of their motives or fear being identified on camera.

High-profile targets

Attacks on foreign journalists, particularly those from Europe, the US and Australia, tend to generate a lot of attention in the international media. Audiences are shocked by violence against supposedly neutral observers. But sometimes militants may use this to their advantage. When *Wall Street Journal* reporter Daniel Pearl was kidnapped in Pakistan in 2002, he had been investigating the relationship between al Qaeda and some Pakistani officials. The militants who kidnapped him accused him of spying and issued a list of their demands via email to the US government before murdering him and releasing a video of his mutilated body. The gruesome nature of the murder and the fact that Pearl was a respected US journalist ensured high levels of media exposure for his killers and their cause. It also led to a variety of media productions, including a Hollywood film called *A Mighty Heart* and a documentary entitled *The Journalist and the Jihadi: The Murder of Daniel Pearl.*

Journalist Daniel Pearl holds up a copy of a newspaper to prove the date in a video made by his kidnappers.

Case study: Anna Politkovskaya

Anna Politkovskaya was a Russian journalist with a reputation for speaking out against her government's human rights abuses. She was particularly outspoken about the war in Chechnya, a region to the south that was trying to break away from Russian rule. Her fame as a journalist and campaigner grew when Chechen terrorists seized control of a theatre in Moscow and she was called in to mediate between the two sides. However, her campaigning led to a series of death threats against her and in October 2006 she was shot dead outside her flat. Some people believe her murder was ordered by Russian officials who objected to her investigations.

Russian journalist Anna Politkovskaya was shot dead in 2006 in the lift of her apartment building.

Silenced and forgotten

Not every journalist has a high profile. Every year, hundreds of reporters, producers, camera crew, drivers and interpreters are threatened or killed in countries around the world and few people know about it. Often they are local journalists, or temporary staff employed on short-term contracts by visiting foreign media. If they are not from a developed country, the national or international media is unlikely to see their deaths as sufficiently interesting. Nearly 200 journalists and media support workers were killed during the war in Iraq. Most of them were Iraqis.

• *Up for discussion* •

During the Iraq war, a US tank fired on a hotel in Baghdad where a number of foreign journalists were staying. US bombs also damaged the offices of the Arab TV channel Al Jazeera. The US military vigorously denied targeting journalists. Why do you think some people refused to believe them?

Look away now

The media has been accused of failing the people of Rwanda (see p.31) by not showing images of the true scale and horror of the killings that took place there in 1994. Yet websites that posted a gruesome video of journalist Daniel Pearl's mutilated body (see p.32) were heavily criticised too. So how should the media respond to extreme images of violence, conflict and war?

Family viewing

Traditional media, such as newspapers, radio, films and TV, have to pay close attention to the expectations of their audiences. TV channels in particular may decide that graphic images of violence are too distressing for 'family' viewing and will choose images that show instead the wounded in hospital, or damage to buildings rather than display dead bodies. However, not all TV channels feel the need to protect the sensitivities of their audiences in this way.

Immune to horror

Some people argue that showing too much video footage of graphic violence and its aftermath can actually lessen its impact. If audiences are exposed to endless scenes of blood-soaked bodies or grief-stricken relatives they may grow tired of such images, or simply become used to them. So editors face a difficult task. They have to balance the often devastating reality of violence in any conflict with their audience's interest in its effects.

A man grieves over the body of his relative after their flat in Gori, Georgia was bombed in 2008.

Case study: 'Precision' bombing

At the beginning of the war in Iraq in 2003, US TV channels tended to show images that suggested a new kind of high-tech warfare fought at a distance, with long-range missiles and precision targeting. The Allies' military press conferences focused on footage of bombs dropping from the air, often at night. However, they did not show the effect of such bombing raids on the ground. Viewers could see buildings, but it was not easy to tell whether they were civilian homes or enemy installations. Arabic TV channels, on the other hand, showed endless images of the dead and dying and also, controversially, pictures of American soldiers captured by the Iraqis. Both approaches clearly served their countries' different interests.

A bomb left over 20 people feared dead beneath the debris of this block of houses in Iraq in 2005.

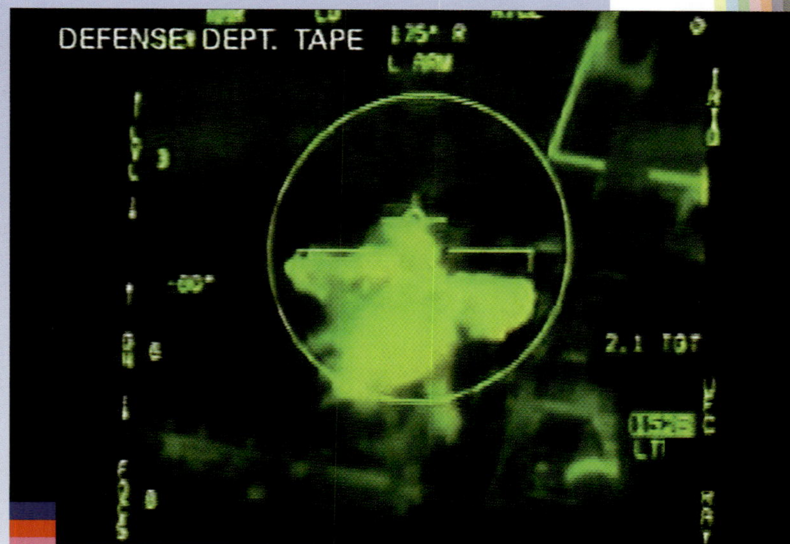

An American plane drops a bomb on a radio relay station in Iraq.

• *Up for discussion* •

In your view, which of the three pictures on these pages is the most memorable?
Can you explain why?
If you were a news editor, what criteria would you use to select images of war?

Public trust

Audiences turn to the media for all sorts of reasons, including entertainment and speculation as well as information. However, in wartime most people want news about what is happening from a source that they can trust. So every news organisation works hard to convince the public that it has the most trustworthy TV channel, radio station or Internet reporting.

Internet versus TV

In many respects, the Internet flourished during the recent war in Iraq. Blogs from soldiers, civilians, warmongers and peacemakers vied for the attention of a worldwide public hungry for news. Nevertheless, viewing statistics also show that people turned to TV for regular updates and coverage of major events such as the capture of Saddam Hussein. This may be because anyone can post a blog without the editorial standards imposed by a TV broadcaster such as the BBC or ABC. Perhaps people turned to blogs for speculation, but preferred TV news for information. Or perhaps they sought reassurance from the presence of a familiar news anchor or well-known journalist.

Journalist Andrew Gilligan (see p.37) arrives to give evidence at the High Court, London.

A disillusioned public

Sometimes public trust in a well-respected news organisation is damaged or shaken. During the Iraq

Case study: Al Jazeera

Al Jazeera is a satellite TV news channel that is partly funded by the government of Qatar. It broadcasts in Arabic and English and has a mainly Middle Eastern/Muslim audience. It came to prominence during the Iraq war, when it broadcast previously unseen footage of al Qaeda leader Osama Bin Laden and proclaimed its independence from the Iraqis as well as the US and its allies. As Muslim communities in western countries such as the US and the UK became more disillusioned with the policies of their governments towards Iraq, they increasingly turned to Al Jazeera for information about the war. However, some analysts think the channel should do more to condemn the activities of Islamic terrorists.

The Al Jazeera news channel rose to international prominence during the Iraq war.

war, a BBC journalist called Andrew Gilligan was accused of misusing the words of a government source (who subsequently committed suicide) to suggest that the government had 'sexed up' its claims about Iraqi Weapons of Mass Destruction (WMDs). During the enquiry that followed, the government was proved wrong about Iraqi WMDs, but the BBC's reputation for accurate reporting was also damaged.

• *Up for discussion* •

Which type of media do you trust the most? Why?
Was Al Jazeera right to show footage of al Qaeda leader Osama Bin Laden?
If so, why?

Dramatising conflict

Films, books, TV dramas and cartoon strips have all been used to tell stories about war. Sometimes the stories are entirely fictional. Often they are based on real events. However, these forms of story-telling serve a different purpose from news bulletins and eyewitness reports. They are designed to entertain and so usually provide audiences with the version of events that they want to see.

Hollywood and war

In the decades after the Second World War, the US film industry tended to glorify the exploits of the Allied forces with a particular emphasis on US heroism. This was very much in line with public opinion. Then, after the war in Vietnam ended in the 1970s, filmmakers began to experiment with a more critical view of war. Films such as *Apocalypse Now* portrayed a much darker, more uncomfortable side to military intervention. However, the recent war in Iraq has been more problematic to dramatise. Films such as *Rendition*, which have been critical of US intervention, have not been box-office hits. This may be because the public feels uncomfortable about such films when soldiers are still fighting.

A still of a scene from *Apocalypse Now*. The darker vision of war that the film offered earned it much critical acclaim.

Revealing the truth?

The problem with dramatising conflict is that it may affect audiences' understanding of what really happened. Films in particular tend to focus on a single viewpoint, with an emphasis on high drama. They may help to humanise conflict, but perhaps they also strengthen popular stereotypes about war, such as the 'lone warrior' or the trigger-happy sniper.

Because there is so little news footage of the massacres in Rwanda in 1994, a film called *Hotel Rwanda* is regarded by many as a valuable source of 'information' about the genocide. It is based on real people and real events, but it is still a dramatisation of the violence.

• Up for discussion •

Do you think it is helpful to dramatise war in books and films? Why? Does it matter if the audience can't always tell what is fiction and what is fact?

Case study: Valley of the Wolves Iraq

A Turkish film called Valley of the Wolves Iraq *was released in 2006 and became a huge box-office hit in Turkey. The film uses a real event as its starting point – the arrest and alleged humiliation of some Turkish special forces by US soldiers in 2003, despite the fact that Turkey and the US were allies. However, the rest of the film is a largely fictional, one-sided account of US cruelty and Turkish revenge. Some critics have expressed concern that the fictionalised elements may provoke racial or religious hatred. Others argue that* Valley of the Wolves Iraq *is no more prejudiced than many Hollywood films about war.*

A Turkish woman stands next to a poster for the movie *Valley of the Wolves Iraq* in Istanbul, 2006.

Media audiences

Wars are fought with words and images as well as guns and bombs. Those who manage the words and the images wield considerable power. They can provoke conflict, control the spread of information, fuel speculation, manipulate public opinion and even, perhaps, help make peace. Sometimes it is journalists, editors and media managers who wield this power. But often the media is influenced by governments, by the military, by ideology or by the very audiences they are trying to satisfy.

24-hour news

We live in an age of instant news, made possible by huge advances in technology. 24-hour news channels need to keep their schedules full of fresh news if they are to hold the interest of their audiences. But this pressure for news can create problems of its own. Programme editors may not wait to check that a breaking news story is accurate because if they delay, their audience may switch to a rival channel. When Private Jessica Lynch was rescued (see p.20) the media did not wait to verify the facts – they simply reported what the military had told them and added some speculation of their own. Most audiences were happy to believe what they were told. Later, when other facts emerged, many felt let down.

Mobile phones make it easy to keep up with breaking news wherever we are.

Case study: Naming the dead

Corporal Sarah Bryant, killed in Afghanistan in 2008.

When Corporal Sarah Bryant became the first female British soldier to be killed in Afghanistan in June 2008, the Daily Mail *newspaper immediately published her name. It was, after all, a big news story. However, there was some doubt as to whether all of Bryant's relatives had been officially informed. The Ministry of Defence asked the BBC to delay publishing her name for a few hours and, despite the news already being available from other sources, the BBC agreed because it said it wanted to respect the sensitivities of the dead soldier's family. Others disagreed, arguing that withholding information was not in the best interests of the BBC or its audiences.*

Finding a balance

The media itself can seem like a battleground, with audiences massed on either side. If we want a more complete understanding of events it is often worth examining what all sides have to say. Truly objective journalism is very difficult to achieve but 'balanced' journalism, where different opinions are aired openly and discussed, is something that we all have a right to expect. What matters is that audiences continue to show that this is what they want.

• *Up for discussion* •

Who do you think has the most power over how the media responds to war and conflict? Is it politicians or the military, or journalists and media managers, or media audiences themselves? What's your view?

Glossary

Allies Countries that fight on the same side in a conflict.

Anti-semitism Fear or hatred of Jews.

Anti-terror laws Laws designed to prevent or intercept terrorist activity.

Atrocities Particularly violent acts, often carried out against a group of civilians.

Balanced reporting Reporting that offers different points of view.

Biased Favouring one viewpoint over another.

Breaking news Fresh news.

Censorship Preventing information from being made public.

Civilian A non-combatant; not a member of the armed forces.

Civil war War between groups of people living in the same country.

Collateral damage A term sometimes used to describe accidental damage to buildings and civilians during a conflict.

Combatant Fighter.

Coverage Reported news.

Demoralise Damage morale.

Deployment Movement of troops.

Displaced civilians Ordinary people who have been forced to leave their homes because of a natural disaster or war.

Editor Someone who makes decisions about the content of a TV programme, website or newspaper.

Embedded reporter A journalist who is assigned to a specific military unit during a conflict.

Ethnic cleansing Ridding an area or a country of a particular ethnic group.

Extremist Someone who holds extreme views, often to do with politics or religion.

Eyewitness Someone who directly observes an event or experiences it themselves.

Fictional Made up; not real.

Free speech Being able to express your opinions without fear of punishment.

Genocide The deliberate murder of a group of people because of their ethnicity or nationality.

Graphic Clearly visible.

Ideology A set of ideas that affect how someone thinks or behaves.

Impartial Not taking sides.

Incite Provoke or encourage.

Leak Provide a news organisation with secret information.

Liberator One who sets others free.

Martyr Someone who dies for their beliefs.

Militant Using violent means to achieve an objective.

Morale Confidence and courage.

News anchor News reader.

News blackout When a news story is blocked or censored.

Objectivity Being fair and impartial.

Photojournalist Someone who photographs news stories.

Press conference An event where journalists receive a news update from the military or politicians and are usually invited to ask questions about it.

Propaganda Using the media to exaggerate or distort the facts so that an audience can be manipulated.

Regime A government, often undemocratic.

Sound bite A phrase or slogan that creates a memorable headline.

Speculate To guess.

Spin An attempt to manipulate the public's understanding of a news story.

Stereotype A fixed idea or impression that may have little basis in reality.

Strategic Intended to achieve a certain aim.

Suicide bomber Someone who blows themselves up in order to kill others.

Tribunal Court hearing to establish the facts.

Unpatriotic Showing a lack of love for your country.

War crime A violent act, such as rape or torture, that goes beyond usual warfare.

War zone Area of conflict.

Warmonger Someone who promotes or pursues war.

Weapons of Mass Destruction Nuclear, chemical or biological weapons that kill in large numbers.

Further information

Books

What's at Issue? War & Conflict by Sean Connolly (Heinemann, 2002)

What's That Got to Do With Me? War and Conflict by Anthony Lishak (Franklin Watts, 2009)

What's Your View? The Power of the Media by Adam Hibbert (Franklin Watts, 2006)

Websites

www.iwm.org.uk/upload/package/29/media war/index.htm
This website contains a wide range of online resources for teachers and students covering techniques and technologies from the First World War to the Iraq War.

www.savedarfur.org
A website that aims to increase public awareness of the conflict in Darfur.

www.unicef.org/infobycountry/index.html
Iraq, Israel, Rwanda, Somalia – click on the country you want to learn more about for quick facts, maps and information.

www.un.org
The United Nations website gives information about its peacekeeping missions all around the world.

Note to parents and teachers: Every effort has been made by the Publishers to ensure that these websites are suitable for children, that they are of the highest educational value, and that they contain no inappropriate or offensive material. However, because of the nature of the Internet, it is impossible to guarantee that the contents of these sites will not be altered. We strongly advise that Internet access is supervised by a responsible adult.

Index

Number in bold refer to captions to illustrations.

These are the list of contents for each title in *Media Power*